50 Zodiac Kitchen Dessert Dishes

By: Kelly Johnson

Table of Contents

- Aries' Fiery Chili Chocolate Lava Cake
- Taurus' Decadent Salted Caramel Cheesecake
- Gemini's Dual-Layered Black & White Mousse
- Cancer's Comforting Warm Apple Crumble
- Leo's Golden Honey Baklava
- Virgo's Elegant Lemon Lavender Tart
- Libra's Perfectly Balanced Raspberry Pistachio Cake
- Scorpio's Mysterious Black Sesame Pudding
- Sagittarius' Exotic Mango Sticky Rice
- Capricorn's Classic Tiramisu
- Aquarius' Unique Blue Spirulina Cheesecake
- Pisces' Dreamy Coconut Cream Pie
- Aries' Bold Red Velvet Cupcakes with Spicy Cream Cheese
- Taurus' Rich Chocolate Hazelnut Tart
- Gemini's Playful Cotton Candy Meringue Kisses
- Cancer's Nostalgic Strawberry Shortcake
- Leo's Show-Stopping Gold Leaf Chocolate Truffles
- Virgo's Naturally Sweet Honey Almond Biscotti
- Libra's Harmonious Dark Chocolate & Cherry Torte
- Scorpio's Intense Espresso Brownies
- Sagittarius' Wanderlust-Inspired Churros with Spiced Chocolate Sauce
- Capricorn's Sophisticated Dark Chocolate & Fig Tart
- Aquarius' Avant-Garde Matcha & Black Sesame Ice Cream
- Pisces' Ethereal Rosewater and Cardamom Rice Pudding
- Aries' Spicy Mexican Hot Chocolate Soufflé
- Taurus' Luxurious Triple Chocolate Mousse
- Gemini's Colorful Rainbow Mille-Feuille
- Cancer's Cozy Cinnamon Sugar Donuts
- Leo's Dramatic Flambéed Cherries Jubilee
- Virgo's Delicate Poached Pears in Red Wine
- Libra's Aesthetic Macaron Tower
- Scorpio's Seductive Red Wine Chocolate Cake
- Sagittarius' Globally Inspired Turkish Delight
- Capricorn's Well-Crafted Classic French Opera Cake
- Aquarius' Inventive Purple Sweet Potato Cheesecake

- Pisces' Ocean-Inspired Blueberry Lemon Sorbet
- Aries' Bold Chili Mango Sorbet
- Taurus' Creamy Peanut Butter Fudge
- Gemini's Funfetti Cake Pops
- Cancer's Warm Peach Cobbler with Vanilla Ice Cream
- Leo's Majestic Saffron and Pistachio Ice Cream
- Virgo's Light & Wholesome Honey Yogurt Parfait
- Libra's Rose Petal and White Chocolate Ganache Tart
- Scorpio's Dark Chocolate Raspberry Coulis Tart
- Sagittarius' Adventurous Cardamom and Orange Blossom Cake
- Capricorn's Refined Almond and Fig Galette
- Aquarius' Unconventional Black Garlic Chocolate Truffles
- Pisces' Soft and Dreamy Angel Food Cake
- Aries' Cinnamon-Spiced Churro Bites
- Taurus' Indulgent Bourbon Pecan Pie

Pisces' Dreamy Coconut Cream Pie

Ingredients:

- 1 pre-baked pie crust
- 1 can (14 oz) coconut milk
- 1 cup whole milk
- ½ cup granulated sugar
- ¼ cup cornstarch
- ¼ tsp salt
- 3 egg yolks
- 1 tsp vanilla extract
- 1 cup shredded coconut
- Whipped cream, for topping

Instructions:

1. In a saucepan over medium heat, whisk together coconut milk, whole milk, sugar, cornstarch, and salt.
2. Cook, stirring, until thickened, about 5 minutes.
3. Whisk egg yolks in a bowl. Gradually add some hot mixture to temper eggs, then return to the pot.
4. Cook until thick, remove from heat, and stir in vanilla and shredded coconut.
5. Pour into the pie crust, let cool, then chill for 3+ hours.
6. Top with whipped cream before serving.

Aries' Fiery Chili Chocolate Lava Cake

Ingredients:

- ½ cup unsalted butter
- 4 oz dark chocolate, chopped
- ½ cup powdered sugar
- 2 eggs
- 2 egg yolks
- ¼ cup flour
- ½ tsp cayenne pepper
- ½ tsp cinnamon
- Pinch of salt

Instructions:

1. Preheat oven to 425°F (220°C). Grease 4 ramekins.
2. Melt butter and chocolate together. Stir in sugar.
3. Whisk in eggs and yolks, then mix in flour, spices, and salt.
4. Divide into ramekins and bake for 10–12 minutes until edges are set but centers are soft.
5. Let cool for 1 minute, then invert onto plates. Serve warm.

Taurus' Decadent Salted Caramel Cheesecake

Ingredients:

- 1½ cups graham cracker crumbs
- ¼ cup melted butter
- 16 oz cream cheese, softened
- ½ cup sugar
- 2 eggs
- 1 tsp vanilla extract
- ½ cup caramel sauce
- ½ tsp sea salt

Instructions:

1. Preheat oven to 325°F (163°C). Mix crumbs and butter, press into a springform pan.
2. Beat cream cheese and sugar until smooth. Add eggs one at a time, then mix in vanilla.
3. Pour over crust and bake for 40 minutes. Let cool.
4. Drizzle with caramel and sprinkle with sea salt before serving.

Gemini's Dual-Layered Black & White Mousse

Ingredients:

- 4 oz dark chocolate
- 4 oz white chocolate
- 2 cups heavy cream, divided
- 2 tbsp sugar
- 1 tsp vanilla extract

Instructions:

1. Melt dark and white chocolate separately. Let cool slightly.
2. Whip 1 cup cream with 1 tbsp sugar, then fold into dark chocolate. Repeat for white chocolate.
3. Layer dark mousse in glasses, then white mousse. Chill for 2+ hours before serving.

Cancer's Comforting Warm Apple Crumble

Ingredients:

- 4 apples, peeled and sliced
- ½ cup brown sugar
- 1 tsp cinnamon
- ½ cup oats
- ½ cup flour
- ¼ cup melted butter

Instructions:

1. Preheat oven to 375°F (190°C). Toss apples with sugar and cinnamon in a baking dish.
2. Mix oats, flour, and butter, then sprinkle over apples.
3. Bake for 30 minutes until golden brown. Serve warm.

Leo's Golden Honey Baklava

Ingredients:

- 1 package phyllo dough
- 1 cup chopped nuts (pistachios or walnuts)
- ½ cup butter, melted
- ½ cup honey
- ¼ cup sugar
- 1 tsp cinnamon

Instructions:

1. Preheat oven to 350°F (175°C).
2. Layer 5 sheets of phyllo, brushing each with butter.
3. Sprinkle nuts and cinnamon, then repeat layers.
4. Cut into diamond shapes and bake for 35 minutes.
5. Drizzle with honey and let soak before serving.

Virgo's Elegant Lemon Lavender Tart

Ingredients:

- 1 tart crust, pre-baked
- ¾ cup lemon juice
- ½ cup sugar
- 3 eggs
- ¼ cup butter, cubed
- 1 tsp dried lavender

Instructions:

1. Whisk lemon juice, sugar, and eggs over medium heat until thick.
2. Remove from heat, stir in butter and lavender.
3. Pour into crust and chill for 3 hours before serving.

Libra's Perfectly Balanced Raspberry Pistachio Cake

Ingredients:

- 1½ cups flour
- 1 tsp baking powder
- ½ cup butter, softened
- ¾ cup sugar
- 2 eggs
- ½ cup milk
- ½ cup ground pistachios
- ½ cup raspberries

Instructions:

1. Preheat oven to 350°F (175°C).
2. Beat butter and sugar, then mix in eggs and milk. Add dry ingredients.
3. Fold in raspberries and pistachios.
4. Bake for 35 minutes, then cool before serving.

Scorpio's Mysterious Black Sesame Pudding

Ingredients:

- 1 cup milk
- ¼ cup black sesame paste
- 2 tbsp sugar
- 2 tbsp cornstarch
- ½ tsp vanilla

Instructions:

1. Heat milk and sesame paste in a saucepan.
2. Whisk sugar and cornstarch, then add to milk.
3. Stir until thickened, then remove from heat and add vanilla.
4. Chill before serving.

Sagittarius' Exotic Mango Sticky Rice

Ingredients:

- 1 cup sticky rice
- 1 cup coconut milk
- ¼ cup sugar
- 1 ripe mango, sliced

Instructions:

1. Cook sticky rice.
2. Heat coconut milk with sugar, then mix with rice.
3. Serve with mango slices.

Capricorn's Classic Tiramisu

Ingredients:

- 1 cup espresso
- 2 tbsp coffee liqueur (optional)
- 12 ladyfingers
- 8 oz mascarpone cheese
- ¼ cup sugar
- 1 cup whipped cream
- Cocoa powder, for dusting

Instructions:

1. Mix espresso and liqueur. Dip ladyfingers and layer in a dish.
2. Beat mascarpone with sugar, then fold in whipped cream.
3. Layer over ladyfingers, then dust with cocoa. Chill overnight.

Aquarius' Unique Blue Spirulina Cheesecake

Ingredients:

- 1½ cups graham cracker crumbs
- ¼ cup melted butter
- 16 oz cream cheese, softened
- ½ cup sugar
- 2 eggs
- 1 tsp vanilla
- 1 tbsp blue spirulina

Instructions:

1. Preheat oven to 325°F (163°C). Mix crumbs and butter, press into a pan.
2. Beat cream cheese and sugar, then mix in eggs, vanilla, and spirulina.
3. Pour over crust and bake for 40 minutes. Chill before serving.

Pisces' Dreamy Coconut Cream Pie

Ingredients:

- 1 pre-baked pie crust
- 1 can (14 oz) coconut milk
- 1 cup whole milk
- ½ cup granulated sugar
- ¼ cup cornstarch
- ¼ tsp salt
- 3 egg yolks
- 1 tsp vanilla extract
- 1 cup shredded coconut
- Whipped cream, for topping

Instructions:

1. In a saucepan over medium heat, whisk together coconut milk, whole milk, sugar, cornstarch, and salt.
2. Cook, stirring, until thickened, about 5 minutes.
3. Whisk egg yolks in a bowl. Gradually add some hot mixture to temper eggs, then return to the pot.
4. Cook until thick, remove from heat, and stir in vanilla and shredded coconut.
5. Pour into the pie crust, let cool, then chill for 3+ hours.
6. Top with whipped cream before serving.

Aries' Bold Red Velvet Cupcakes with Spicy Cream Cheese

Ingredients:

- 1 ¼ cups flour
- 1 tbsp cocoa powder
- ½ tsp baking soda
- ½ cup unsalted butter, softened
- ¾ cup sugar
- 1 egg
- ½ cup buttermilk
- 1 tsp vanilla extract
- 1 tbsp red food coloring

Spicy Cream Cheese Frosting:

- 8 oz cream cheese, softened
- ½ cup butter, softened
- 2 cups powdered sugar
- ½ tsp cayenne pepper
- ½ tsp cinnamon

Instructions:

1. Preheat oven to 350°F (175°C) and line a cupcake tin.
2. Whisk dry ingredients. In a separate bowl, beat butter and sugar until fluffy.
3. Add egg, vanilla, and red food coloring.
4. Alternate adding dry ingredients and buttermilk, mixing just until combined.
5. Divide into liners and bake for 18 minutes. Cool completely.
6. For frosting, beat all ingredients until smooth. Pipe onto cupcakes.

Taurus' Rich Chocolate Hazelnut Tart

Ingredients:

- 1 ½ cups crushed chocolate cookies
- ¼ cup melted butter
- 1 cup heavy cream
- 8 oz dark chocolate, chopped
- ½ cup hazelnut spread
- ½ cup chopped hazelnuts

Instructions:

1. Mix cookie crumbs with melted butter and press into a tart pan. Chill.
2. Heat heavy cream until warm, then pour over chocolate. Stir until melted.
3. Mix in hazelnut spread, then pour into the crust.
4. Sprinkle hazelnuts on top and chill for 3+ hours before serving.

Gemini's Playful Cotton Candy Meringue Kisses

Ingredients:

- 3 egg whites
- ¾ cup sugar
- ¼ tsp cream of tartar
- ½ tsp cotton candy extract
- Blue and pink food coloring

Instructions:

1. Preheat oven to 200°F (95°C). Line a baking sheet.
2. Beat egg whites until foamy. Add cream of tartar.
3. Gradually add sugar and continue beating until stiff peaks form.
4. Stir in cotton candy extract.
5. Divide batter and color one half blue, one pink.
6. Pipe into small kisses and bake for 1½ hours. Turn off oven and let cool inside.

Cancer's Nostalgic Strawberry Shortcake

Ingredients:

- 2 cups flour
- ¼ cup sugar
- 1 tbsp baking powder
- ½ cup cold butter, cubed
- ¾ cup heavy cream
- 2 cups fresh strawberries, sliced
- ¼ cup sugar
- 1 cup whipped cream

Instructions:

1. Preheat oven to 400°F (200°C). Mix flour, sugar, and baking powder.
2. Cut in butter until crumbly. Add cream and mix to form a dough.
3. Pat into rounds and bake for 15 minutes.
4. Toss strawberries with sugar and let sit for 10 minutes.
5. Slice shortcakes, fill with strawberries and whipped cream.

Leo's Show-Stopping Gold Leaf Chocolate Truffles

Ingredients:

- 8 oz dark chocolate, chopped
- ½ cup heavy cream
- 1 tbsp butter
- 1 tsp vanilla extract
- Gold leaf sheets

Instructions:

1. Heat cream and butter until warm, then pour over chocolate. Stir until smooth.
2. Mix in vanilla and chill until firm.
3. Roll into balls and place on parchment paper.
4. Carefully apply gold leaf to each truffle using tweezers.
5. Store in the fridge until ready to serve.

Virgo's Naturally Sweet Honey Almond Biscotti

Ingredients:

- 2 cups flour
- 1 tsp baking powder
- ½ tsp salt
- ½ cup honey
- ¼ cup melted butter
- 2 eggs
- 1 tsp vanilla
- ½ cup sliced almonds

Instructions:

1. Preheat oven to 350°F (175°C). Line a baking sheet.
2. Mix flour, baking powder, and salt.
3. Stir in honey, butter, eggs, and vanilla until combined.
4. Fold in almonds and shape dough into a log.
5. Bake for 25 minutes. Cool, then slice into biscotti and bake for another 15 minutes.

Libra's Harmonious Dark Chocolate & Cherry Torte

Ingredients:

- 1 cup dark chocolate, melted
- ½ cup butter
- ¾ cup sugar
- 3 eggs
- ½ cup flour
- ½ cup cherry preserves

Instructions:

1. Preheat oven to 350°F (175°C).
2. Beat butter and sugar until fluffy, then add eggs one at a time.
3. Stir in melted chocolate and flour.
4. Pour half the batter into a greased pan, spread cherry preserves, then top with remaining batter.
5. Bake for 30 minutes. Let cool before serving.

Scorpio's Intense Espresso Brownies

Ingredients:

- ½ cup butter
- 1 cup sugar
- 2 eggs
- 1 tsp vanilla
- ½ cup flour
- ¼ cup cocoa powder
- 1 tbsp instant espresso powder
- ¼ tsp salt

Instructions:

1. Preheat oven to 350°F (175°C). Line a baking pan.
2. Melt butter, then stir in sugar.
3. Whisk in eggs and vanilla.
4. Sift in flour, cocoa, espresso, and salt.
5. Pour into pan and bake for 20 minutes.
6. Let cool, then cut into squares.

Sagittarius' Wanderlust-Inspired Churros with Spiced Chocolate Sauce

Ingredients:

For the churros:

- 1 cup water
- 2 ½ tbsp sugar
- ½ tsp salt
- 2 tbsp butter
- 1 cup flour
- 1 egg
- ½ tsp vanilla extract
- Vegetable oil, for frying
- ½ cup sugar + 1 tsp cinnamon (for coating)

For the spiced chocolate sauce:

- ½ cup heavy cream
- 4 oz dark chocolate, chopped
- ½ tsp cinnamon
- ¼ tsp cayenne pepper

Instructions:

1. In a saucepan, bring water, sugar, salt, and butter to a boil.
2. Remove from heat and stir in flour until it forms a dough.
3. Let cool slightly, then mix in egg and vanilla.
4. Heat oil to 375°F (190°C). Pipe dough into hot oil, frying until golden. Drain and coat in cinnamon sugar.
5. Heat cream, then pour over chocolate. Stir in spices until smooth. Serve churros with sauce.

Capricorn's Sophisticated Dark Chocolate & Fig Tart

Ingredients:

- 1 ½ cups crushed chocolate cookies
- ¼ cup melted butter
- 8 oz dark chocolate, chopped
- ¾ cup heavy cream
- 2 tbsp honey
- 5 fresh figs, sliced

Instructions:

1. Mix cookie crumbs with butter and press into a tart pan. Chill.
2. Heat cream, then pour over chocolate. Stir in honey until smooth.
3. Pour into the crust and chill for 3+ hours.
4. Arrange fig slices on top before serving.

Aquarius' Avant-Garde Matcha & Black Sesame Ice Cream

Ingredients:

- 2 cups heavy cream
- 1 cup whole milk
- ¾ cup sugar
- 4 egg yolks
- 1 tbsp matcha powder
- ¼ cup black sesame paste

Instructions:

1. Heat cream and milk until warm.
2. Whisk yolks and sugar, then slowly add warm milk to temper.
3. Return to heat and cook until thickened.
4. Divide mixture in half—stir matcha into one, sesame paste into the other.
5. Chill both, then swirl together before churning in an ice cream maker.

Pisces' Ethereal Rosewater and Cardamom Rice Pudding

Ingredients:

- ½ cup basmati rice
- 2 cups whole milk
- ½ cup heavy cream
- ⅓ cup sugar
- ½ tsp ground cardamom
- 1 tsp rosewater
- ¼ cup chopped pistachios

Instructions:

1. Simmer rice, milk, cream, sugar, and cardamom until thick, about 30 minutes.
2. Stir in rosewater and let cool.
3. Garnish with pistachios before serving.

Aries' Spicy Mexican Hot Chocolate Soufflé

Ingredients:

- 4 oz dark chocolate, chopped
- 2 tbsp butter
- 2 tbsp flour
- ½ cup milk
- ¼ cup sugar
- 1 tsp cinnamon
- ¼ tsp cayenne
- 2 egg yolks
- 3 egg whites

Instructions:

1. Preheat oven to 375°F (190°C). Grease ramekins.
2. Melt butter and flour, whisk in milk until thickened.
3. Stir in chocolate, cinnamon, cayenne, and yolks.
4. Beat whites with sugar to stiff peaks. Fold into chocolate mixture.
5. Bake for 15 minutes and serve immediately.

Taurus' Luxurious Triple Chocolate Mousse

Ingredients:

- 4 oz dark chocolate
- 4 oz milk chocolate
- 4 oz white chocolate
- 1 ½ cups heavy cream, divided
- 3 egg yolks
- 3 egg whites
- 3 tbsp sugar

Instructions:

1. Melt each chocolate separately, stirring in ½ egg yolk each.
2. Beat heavy cream to soft peaks and divide into three.
3. Beat egg whites with sugar to stiff peaks and divide into three.
4. Fold cream and whites into each chocolate, then layer in glasses.
5. Chill before serving.

Gemini's Colorful Rainbow Mille-Feuille

Ingredients:

- 1 sheet puff pastry
- 1 cup pastry cream
- Food coloring (red, orange, yellow, green, blue, purple)
- ½ cup powdered sugar

Instructions:

1. Bake puff pastry at 375°F (190°C) until golden, then cool.
2. Divide pastry cream into six bowls and color each one.
3. Cut pastry into equal rectangles and layer with different colored creams.
4. Dust with powdered sugar before serving.

Cancer's Cozy Cinnamon Sugar Donuts

Ingredients:

- 2 cups flour
- 1 tsp baking powder
- ½ tsp salt
- ½ cup sugar
- ½ cup milk
- 1 egg
- 2 tbsp melted butter
- 1 tsp vanilla
- ½ cup sugar + 1 tbsp cinnamon (for coating)

Instructions:

1. Preheat oil to 350°F (175°C).
2. Mix flour, baking powder, salt, and sugar.
3. Stir in milk, egg, butter, and vanilla until a dough forms.
4. Roll out, cut donuts, and fry until golden.
5. Coat in cinnamon sugar before serving.

Leo's Dramatic Flambéed Cherries Jubilee

Ingredients:

- 2 cups fresh cherries, pitted
- ½ cup sugar
- ¼ cup brandy
- 1 tbsp butter
- 1 tsp vanilla
- Vanilla ice cream (for serving)

Instructions:

1. In a pan, heat cherries, sugar, and butter until softened.
2. Add brandy and ignite carefully. Let flames die down.
3. Stir in vanilla and serve over ice cream.

Virgo's Delicate Poached Pears in Red Wine

Ingredients:

- 4 firm pears, peeled
- 2 cups red wine
- ¾ cup sugar
- 1 cinnamon stick
- 2 star anise
- 1 vanilla bean (or 1 tsp vanilla extract)
- Zest of 1 orange

Instructions:

1. In a saucepan, combine wine, sugar, cinnamon, star anise, vanilla, and orange zest. Bring to a simmer.
2. Add pears and simmer for 25-30 minutes, turning occasionally, until tender.
3. Remove pears and reduce the liquid into a syrup.
4. Serve pears drizzled with syrup.

Libra's Aesthetic Macaron Tower

Ingredients:

- 1 ¾ cups almond flour
- 1 ¾ cups powdered sugar
- 3 egg whites
- ½ cup granulated sugar
- Food coloring (as desired)
- 1 cup buttercream (various flavors for layering)

Instructions:

1. Sift almond flour and powdered sugar together.
2. Beat egg whites until foamy, then gradually add granulated sugar, beating until stiff peaks form.
3. Fold in dry ingredients gently and add food coloring.
4. Pipe circles onto a lined baking sheet and let sit for 30 minutes.
5. Bake at 300°F (150°C) for 12-15 minutes.
6. Fill with buttercream and arrange into a tower shape.

Scorpio's Seductive Red Wine Chocolate Cake

Ingredients:

- 1 ¾ cups flour
- ¾ cup cocoa powder
- 1 ½ tsp baking soda
- ½ tsp salt
- 1 cup sugar
- ½ cup butter, softened
- 2 eggs
- 1 tsp vanilla
- 1 cup red wine
- ½ cup sour cream

Instructions:

1. Preheat oven to 350°F (175°C). Grease a cake pan.
2. Mix flour, cocoa, baking soda, and salt.
3. Beat butter and sugar, then add eggs and vanilla.
4. Alternately add wine and sour cream with the dry ingredients.
5. Pour into the pan and bake for 30-35 minutes.

Sagittarius' Globally Inspired Turkish Delight

Ingredients:

- 4 cups sugar
- 1 ¼ cups cornstarch
- 4 ½ cups water
- 1 tsp lemon juice
- 1 tbsp rose water
- 1 tsp vanilla
- ½ cup chopped pistachios (optional)
- Powdered sugar (for dusting)

Instructions:

1. Boil sugar, lemon juice, and 1 ½ cups water until dissolved.
2. In a separate pot, mix cornstarch with remaining water and cook until thick.
3. Gradually add sugar syrup, stirring continuously.
4. Simmer for 45-60 minutes, then add rose water, vanilla, and pistachios.
5. Pour into a greased dish and set overnight.
6. Cut into cubes and dust with powdered sugar.

Capricorn's Well-Crafted Classic French Opera Cake

Ingredients:

- 6 egg whites
- ½ cup sugar
- 1 cup almond flour
- ½ cup flour
- ¼ cup butter, melted
- ½ cup coffee syrup
- 1 cup ganache (chocolate + cream)
- 1 cup coffee buttercream
- 8 oz dark chocolate (for glaze)

Instructions:

1. Whip egg whites and sugar into stiff peaks. Fold in almond flour and melted butter.
2. Bake in a thin layer at 375°F (190°C) for 10-12 minutes.
3. Brush with coffee syrup and layer with ganache and buttercream.
4. Chill, then top with a glossy dark chocolate glaze.

Aquarius' Inventive Purple Sweet Potato Cheesecake

Ingredients:

- 1 ½ cups graham cracker crumbs
- ¼ cup melted butter
- 8 oz cream cheese
- ¾ cup sugar
- 1 cup mashed purple sweet potato
- ½ tsp vanilla
- 2 eggs

Instructions:

1. Mix crumbs and butter, pressing into a cheesecake pan.
2. Blend cream cheese, sugar, sweet potato, and vanilla. Add eggs one at a time.
3. Pour over crust and bake at 325°F (160°C) for 50 minutes.
4. Cool before serving.

Pisces' Ocean-Inspired Blueberry Lemon Sorbet

Ingredients:

- 2 cups blueberries
- ½ cup sugar
- ½ cup water
- Juice of 1 lemon
- Zest of 1 lemon

Instructions:

1. Simmer blueberries, sugar, and water until soft.
2. Blend, then strain. Stir in lemon juice and zest.
3. Freeze, stirring every 30 minutes until set.

Aries' Bold Chili Mango Sorbet

Ingredients:

- 3 ripe mangoes, diced
- ½ cup sugar
- Juice of 1 lime
- ½ tsp chili powder

Instructions:

1. Blend all ingredients until smooth.
2. Freeze, stirring every 30 minutes until set.

Taurus' Creamy Peanut Butter Fudge

Ingredients:

- 2 cups sugar
- ½ cup milk
- 1 cup peanut butter
- 1 tsp vanilla

Instructions:

1. Heat sugar and milk to a boil for 2-3 minutes.
2. Remove from heat and stir in peanut butter and vanilla.
3. Pour into a dish and set before cutting into squares.

Gemini's Funfetti Cake Pops

Ingredients:

- 1 box vanilla cake mix
- ½ cup frosting
- 1 cup white chocolate, melted
- Sprinkles

Instructions:

1. Bake cake as directed, then crumble and mix with frosting.
2. Roll into balls and chill.
3. Dip in melted chocolate and top with sprinkles.

Cancer's Warm Peach Cobbler with Vanilla Ice Cream

Ingredients:

- 4 peaches, sliced
- ½ cup sugar
- 1 tsp cinnamon
- 1 cup flour
- 1 tsp baking powder
- ½ cup milk
- ½ cup butter, melted

Instructions:

1. Preheat oven to 350°F (175°C).
2. Toss peaches with sugar and cinnamon.
3. Mix flour, baking powder, and milk.
4. Pour melted butter into a baking dish, then layer batter and peaches.
5. Bake for 40 minutes and serve with ice cream.

Leo's Majestic Saffron and Pistachio Ice Cream

Ingredients:

- 2 cups heavy cream
- 1 cup whole milk
- ¾ cup sugar
- 1 tsp saffron threads
- ½ tsp cardamom powder
- 4 egg yolks
- ½ cup chopped pistachios

Instructions:

1. Heat milk, cream, sugar, and saffron over low heat until warm.
2. Whisk egg yolks and gradually temper with warm milk mixture.
3. Return to heat and cook until thickened.
4. Stir in cardamom and pistachios. Chill and churn in an ice cream maker.

Virgo's Light & Wholesome Honey Yogurt Parfait

Ingredients:

- 2 cups Greek yogurt
- ¼ cup honey
- 1 cup granola
- 1 cup mixed berries

Instructions:

1. Layer yogurt, honey, granola, and berries in a glass.
2. Repeat layers and serve immediately.

Libra's Rose Petal and White Chocolate Ganache Tart

Ingredients:

- 1 pre-baked tart shell
- 8 oz white chocolate
- ½ cup heavy cream
- 1 tbsp rose water
- 2 tbsp edible rose petals

Instructions:

1. Heat cream, pour over white chocolate, and stir until smooth.
2. Add rose water and pour into tart shell.
3. Garnish with rose petals and chill until set.

Scorpio's Dark Chocolate Raspberry Coulis Tart

Ingredients:

- 1 pre-baked chocolate tart shell
- 8 oz dark chocolate
- ½ cup heavy cream
- ½ cup raspberry puree
- 2 tbsp sugar

Instructions:

1. Heat cream and pour over chocolate. Stir until smooth.
2. Pour into tart shell and let set.
3. Drizzle raspberry coulis over tart before serving.

Sagittarius' Adventurous Cardamom and Orange Blossom Cake

Ingredients:

- 1 ½ cups flour
- 1 tsp baking powder
- ½ tsp salt
- 1 tsp cardamom
- ½ cup butter, softened
- ¾ cup sugar
- 2 eggs
- ½ cup milk
- 1 tsp orange blossom water

Instructions:

1. Preheat oven to 350°F (175°C).
2. Mix dry ingredients. Cream butter and sugar, then add eggs.
3. Alternate adding dry ingredients and milk. Stir in orange blossom water.
4. Bake for 30 minutes.

Capricorn's Refined Almond and Fig Galette

Ingredients:

- 1 sheet puff pastry
- ½ cup almond flour
- ¼ cup sugar
- 1 egg
- 6 fresh figs, sliced

Instructions:

1. Preheat oven to 375°F (190°C).
2. Mix almond flour, sugar, and egg. Spread onto pastry.
3. Arrange figs and fold edges.
4. Bake for 30 minutes.

Aquarius' Unconventional Black Garlic Chocolate Truffles

Ingredients:

- 8 oz dark chocolate
- ½ cup heavy cream
- 1 tbsp mashed black garlic
- Cocoa powder for rolling

Instructions:

1. Heat cream, stir in black garlic, and pour over chocolate. Stir until smooth.
2. Chill until firm, roll into balls, and coat in cocoa powder.

Pisces' Soft and Dreamy Angel Food Cake

Ingredients:

- 1 cup cake flour
- 1 ½ cups sugar
- 12 egg whites
- 1 tsp cream of tartar
- 1 tsp vanilla

Instructions:

1. Preheat oven to 350°F (175°C).
2. Beat egg whites with cream of tartar until soft peaks form.
3. Gradually add sugar, then fold in flour and vanilla.
4. Pour into an ungreased tube pan and bake for 40 minutes.

Aries' Cinnamon-Spiced Churro Bites

Ingredients:

- 1 cup water
- ½ cup butter
- 1 cup flour
- 2 eggs
- 1 tsp cinnamon
- ¼ cup sugar
- Oil for frying

Instructions:

1. Boil water and butter. Stir in flour until a dough forms.
2. Remove from heat, add eggs one at a time.
3. Pipe into hot oil and fry until golden.
4. Toss in cinnamon-sugar.

Taurus' Indulgent Bourbon Pecan Pie

Ingredients:

- 1 pie crust
- 1 cup pecans
- ¾ cup corn syrup
- ½ cup brown sugar
- 3 eggs
- 2 tbsp bourbon
- 1 tsp vanilla

Instructions:

1. Preheat oven to 350°F (175°C).
2. Whisk syrup, sugar, eggs, bourbon, and vanilla.
3. Pour over pecans in the crust and bake for 50 minutes.